Need to Know
Tobacco

Sean Connolly

Heinemann

www.heinemann.co.uk
visit our website to find out more information about **Heinemann Library** books.

To order:

 Phone 44 (0) 1865 888066

Send a fax to 44 (0) 1865 314091

Visit the Heinemann Bookshop at www.heinemann.co.uk to browse our catalogue and order online.

First published in Great Britain by Heinemann Library, Halley Court, Jordan Hill, Oxford OX2 8EJ,
a division of Reed Educational and Professional Publishing Ltd.

Heinemann is a registered trademark of Reed Educational & Professional Publishing Limited.

Oxford Melbourne Auckland Johannesburg Blantyre Gaborone Ibadan Portsmouth NH (USA) Chicago

Designed by M2 Graphic Design
Printed in Hong Kong / China
Originated by Ambassador Litho Ltd.

ISBN 0431 097801 (hardback)   ISBN 0431 097909 (paperback)
04 03 02 01   05 04 03 02 01
10 9 8 7 6 5 4 3 2   10 9 8 7 6 5 4 3 2 1

British Library Cataloguing in Publication Data
Sean Connolly
Tobacco – (Need to know)
1. Smoking – Juvenile literature 2. Tobacco habit – Juvenile literature 3. Tobacco – Physiological effect –
Juvenile literature I. Title 362.2' 96

Acknowledgements
The Publishers would like to thank the following for permission to reproduce photographs: Advertising
Archive: pg.36, pg.39; Camera Press: pg.5, pg.11, pg.23, pg.29; Corbis: pg.10; Format: pg.26, pg.31,
pg.37, pg.47; Gareth Boden: pg.49; Hulton Getty: pg.22; Magnum Photos: Ara Guler pg.24, Michael K
Nichols pg.25, Ron Benvenisti pg.27; Network: pg.8, pg.9, pg.17, pg.41, pg.45; NHPA: pg.6; Peter Newark:
pg.21; Photoedit: pg.35; Photofusion: pg.7, pg.16, pg.33, pg.48, pg.51, pg.,53; Rex Features: pg.13;
Science Photo Library: pg.14, pg.15, pg.19, pg.30, pg.43, pg.43, pg.46.

Cover photograph reproduced with permission of Science Photo Library.

Every effort has been made to contact copyright holders of any material reproduced in this book.
Any omissions will be rectified in subsequent printings if notice is given to the publisher.

Any words appearing in the text in bold, **like this**, are explained in the Glossary..

Contents

Introduction	4
What is tobacco?	6
Part of society	10
Is smoking addictive?	12
Life with smoking	16
Tobacco's history	20
Public reaction	24
Who smokes and why?	26
Across the generations	30
The initial cost	34
The tobacco industry	36
The world market	40
The 'other' tobacco industry	42
Legal matters	44
Treatment and counselling	46
Giving up	48
People to talk to	50
Information and advice	52
Glossary	54
Index	56

Introduction

The public spends a great deal of time, money and energy in its fight against the spread of illegal drugs such as heroin and cocaine. This is no bad thing, since these drugs – and others like them – cause misery, increased crime and sometimes death. But in this 'war on drugs' it is too easy to overlook some perfectly legal drugs that cause as much damage or more. Alcohol is one: tobacco is another.

Misplaced glamour

People have been fascinated by tobacco since it was first brought back to Europe by explorers some five hundred years ago. Even then it was clear that this substance had the power to keep people using it, no matter what the consequences. There were also those who criticized tobacco fiercely, recognizing some of the more obvious health risks associated with it.

Even today many people are captivated by the smoke of this plant and smoking is portrayed as glamorous and sexy. People who get caught in its spell find it hard to explain what it is that keeps them smoking – it relaxes some people, it fires others up, still others need it to deal with stress. What these people are experiencing, however, are textbook examples of **dependence** on a drug. The drug in this case is nicotine.

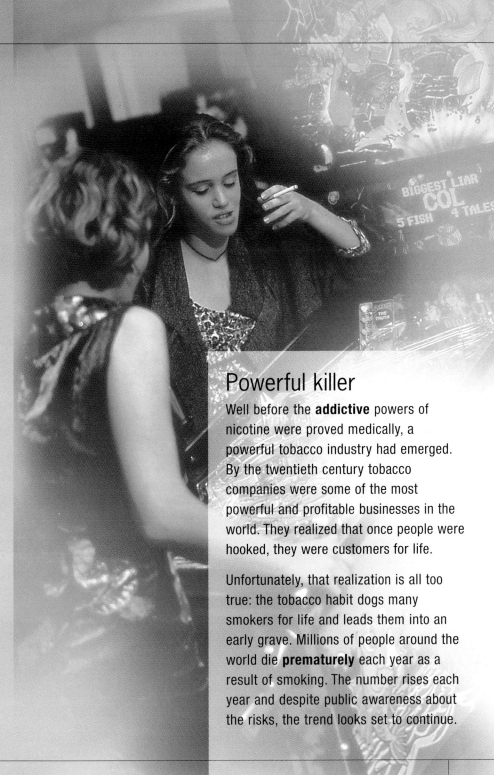

Powerful killer

Well before the **addictive** powers of nicotine were proved medically, a powerful tobacco industry had emerged. By the twentieth century tobacco companies were some of the most powerful and profitable businesses in the world. They realized that once people were hooked, they were customers for life.

Unfortunately, that realization is all too true: the tobacco habit dogs many smokers for life and leads them into an early grave. Millions of people around the world die **prematurely** each year as a result of smoking. The number rises each year and despite public awareness about the risks, the trend looks set to continue.

What is tobacco?

Tobacco comes from the dried leaves of the plant **genus** *Nicotiana*. The most commonly harvested species of this genus is *Nicotiana tabacum*, which is native only to North and South America. Tobacco contains an 'active ingredient' – nicotine – which is the drug that leads to **dependence** among smokers and other users of tobacco.

Different tastes

Tobacco is **processed** in different ways and reaches the consumer in many varieties. The most common form of processed tobacco is the cigarette, which has dominated world markets since the beginning of the twentieth century. Different strains of the tobacco plant, coupled with varying techniques for **curing** the leaves, produce a range of tastes for cigarettes. In the United States and the UK, for example, the most popular brands of cigarette are described as 'blond', which refers to the lighter taste that comes from Virginia tobacco. Smokers in other countries in continental Europe, such as France, prefer the 'darker' flavour of cigarettes associated with their oriental flavouring.

Tastes in the type of cigarette being smoked reflect changing fashions as much as different cultural influences.

Tobacco farming is an important economic activity in many US States.

In the United States and the UK, most cigarettes have filter tips, with the filters being made up largely of stems and sweepings that are otherwise discarded in the manufacturing process. As recently as twenty years ago, though, many American and British smokers bought large quantities of unfiltered cigarettes or loose tobacco, which they would then roll up themselves.

Underlying mystery

Most of the effect of smoking is due to the active ingredient, nicotine. What the smokers get from the nicotine remains unclear, however. People who smoke regularly do so for many different reasons, the most obvious being that they are compelled by a dependence on the nicotine, in the same way that a heavy drinker is **dependent** on alcohol. The many psychological reactions that smokers ascribe to the habit, however, suggest a range of other reasons, perhaps partly linked to this sense of dependence.

Strictly speaking, nicotine is a mild **stimulant**, and its effects would normally be expected to provide a boost in the form of extra energy and alertness. Smokers, however, note a range of other reactions to the drug. Some people would say that smoking calms them down in tense situations. Others find that the activity is stimulating and makes them feel more creative. Yet others simply feel that smoking takes their minds off other problems

What is tobacco?

About 40 years ago, psychologists tried to unravel the complex and contradictory mystery about the attraction of smoking. They concluded that smoking provided a type of oral **gratification**. Simply holding the cigarette in the mouth provided comfort. More recently, theories about why people smoke have become more complicated and many scientists believe that there is a **genetic** reason for people smoking.

A dangerous habit

There is widespread medical agreement about how dangerous smoking is. The health risks, which are discussed in more detail later in this book, range from heart disease to a wide variety of respiratory illnesses such as emphysema. Smoking can also lead to a number of cancers, most commonly lung cancer. In addition to triggering these **fatal** diseases, smoking hastens the ageing process: many smokers develop lined faces long before non-smokers of the same age. Even those who do not smoke themselves can be at risk from the smoke exhaled by those around them. Inhaling smoke in this way is called **passive smoking**.

A choice of poisons

People can take tobacco in many forms. Smoking, in the form of cigarettes, cigars and pipe tobacco, is the most common. The last two forms are sometimes considered less dangerous than cigarettes because most smokers of cigars and pipes do not inhale the tobacco smoke into their lungs. Tobacco can also be chewed or sniffed into the nostrils (when it is called snuff).

Part of society

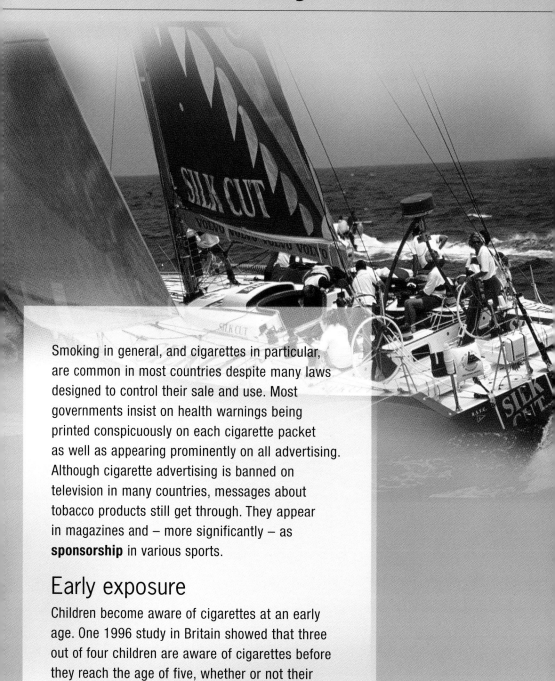

Smoking in general, and cigarettes in particular, are common in most countries despite many laws designed to control their sale and use. Most governments insist on health warnings being printed conspicuously on each cigarette packet as well as appearing prominently on all advertising. Although cigarette advertising is banned on television in many countries, messages about tobacco products still get through. They appear in magazines and – more significantly – as **sponsorship** in various sports.

Early exposure

Children become aware of cigarettes at an early age. One 1996 study in Britain showed that three out of four children are aware of cigarettes before they reach the age of five, whether or not their parents smoke.

By the age of eleven, one-third of children had experimented with smoking; the figure rises to two-thirds of all sixteen-year-olds.

Despite the restrictions on tobacco advertising and widespread health campaigns about the dangers of smoking, children regularly take up smoking. Some experts suggest that young people may believe that the health warnings do not apply to them – only to older people.

American studies indicate that the problem of young people smoking is not just serious, but getting worse. In 1991, about 14 per cent of thirteen-year-olds, 20 per cent of fifteen-year-olds and 28 per cent of seventeen-year-olds had smoked within the past month. By 1995 the figures had risen to 19 per cent, 27 per cent and 34 per cent repectively.

Put that in your pipe...

Young people – boys in particular – are especially influenced by sports-related advertising. Formula One motor racing, which has long links with the tobacco industry, is a good example. A 1997 report in the British medical journal *The Lancet* found evidence that boys whose favourite sport was motor racing were twice as likely to become regular smokers as boys who had no interest in the sport.

Some countries, such as the UK, have introduced measures to ban tobacco advertising in sports such as Formula One motor racing.

Is smoking addictive?

The quick answer is 'yes'. In any discussion of **addiction**, however, medical researchers prefer to use the word **dependence** to describe the compulsion to use a substance, usually a drug. Dependence, in turn, is usually divided into two categories: physical and psychological. A drug is said to cause physical dependence if the user continually needs to increase the dose to maintain the effects of the drug – a pattern called **tolerance** – and then suffers **withdrawal** symptoms when it is stopped. Alcohol and heroin are good examples of drugs that cause physical dependence. Tobacco, through its active ingredient nicotine, fits this description. Studies have shown that people rapidly build up a tolerance to the effects of nicotine. First-time smokers experience a range of unpleasant effects, such as dizziness and nausea, but these lessen as the person continues to smoke. Sometimes, the unpleasant effects have disappeared within a few days.

Nicotine is a **stimulant**. Noting this fact, medical researchers gave a group of smokers equal doses of nicotine one hour apart. The heart rates of the group increased each time – one signal of a stimulant at work – but it happened much more after the first dose than after the second. Tolerance was demonstrated even in the short term.

Send for reinforcements

Smoking, or nicotine intake, also scores highly on the psychological dependence scale. The dependence builds alongside the production of certain chemicals in the brain. Nicotine triggers the release of dopamine, a chemical in the brain that is associated with feelings of pleasure. Nevertheless, recent research has shown that in the long term nicotine actually suppresses the ability of the brain to experience pleasure. Because of this, smokers need greater amounts of nicotine to achieve the same level of pleasure.

Psychologists use the term **reinforcer** to describe something that drives an individual to seek more. Nicotine acts as a reinforcer in the way it motivates people to smoke more. The same effect is noticeable in laboratory rats, which will press a bar in order to obtain a supply of nicotine.

Young people can be affected by the dependence process just as strongly as adults. In a 1991 study, nearly two-thirds of smokers aged from eleven to fifteen said that they would have difficulty in getting through a week without smoking. Three-quarters of these smokers said that they would find it hard to give up smoking altogether.

Often seen as less harmful than cigarette smoking, regular cigar smoking can also lead to serious illnesses.

Is smoking addictive?

Coming off

Withdrawal symptoms play a large part in keeping people hooked on a drug. Nicotine withdrawal is unpleasant and many would-be quitters fall at this first hurdle. Symptoms include an intense craving for cigarettes (the craving is actually for nicotine), irritability, anxiety, poor concentration, restlessness, decreased heart rate and weight gain. Some people have argued that these symptoms really relate to stopping the activity of smoking, not the withdrawal from nicotine itself. However, experiments have shown that the symptoms disappear if people get nicotine in another form (such as gum or patches). The symptoms remain if the same people receive a **placebo** that does not contain nicotine.

❝I want to hurt something.❞

(Anonymous smoker experiencing nicotine withdrawal, quoted in *Buzzed*)

"Over the past decade there has been increasing recognition that underlying smoking behaviour and its remarkable intractability to change is addiction to the drug nicotine. Nicotine has been shown to have effects on the brain's dopamine systems similar to those of heroin and cocaine."

(The UK Government's Scientific Committee on Tobacco and Health, 1998)

Nicotine patches worn on the skin help some smokers to kick the tobacco habit.

Life with smoking

By the time most people have become regular smokers, the reasons that drove them to start – thinking it is sexy or cool, or perhaps a way of losing weight – are largely forgotten. Other more negative factors begin to emerge in the short term. These include the depressing realization that the smoking habit is expensive, the awareness that smoking can affect the way they look and the decreased resistance to certain illnesses. Over the longer term, smokers need to face the prospect of more serious, possibly life-threatening diseases linked with smoking. It is at that stage that the 'way of life' can become a 'way of death'.

All in appearance

Tobacco can affect a person's appearance by altering the skin, the body shape and weight. These changes are not in themselves life-threatening but they can, nevertheless, increase the risk of more serious ailments. What is more, they have a noticeable ageing effect on the body.

Advertising images such as that of the 'Marlboro Man' are aimed to promote a rugged, healthy impression of smoking.

Tobacco affects the skin in two ways. The smoke that is exhaled or that drifts from the tip of the cigarette dries the surface of the skin. Smoking also restricts the flow in the body's blood vessels, so that less blood flows to the skin. Some researchers suggest that smoking reduces the body's supplies of vitamin A, which protects against some of these skin-damaging effects. When skin is damaged by smoke it acquires a greyish, wasted appearance. It has less elastin, the protein that keeps skin **supple**. As a result regular smokers in their forties have as many wrinkles on their face as non-smokers in their sixties. In addition to the issue of ageing, tobacco is linked with a much higher likelihood of developing psoriasis, an uncomfortable and unsightly skin ailment.

Smoking also affects the shape of the person's body. While it is true that the **stimulant** nature of nicotine means that many smokers are thinner than their non-smoking counterparts, their bodies store fats in unusual places. Smokers are more likely to store fat around the waist and upper torso. This can cause an imbalance in the waist-to-hip ratio (WHR), which is a measure of overall health. People with a high WHR run a greater risk of developing high blood pressure, diabetes, heart disease and – in women – cancer of the womb and breast.

The last stage

The ultimate way of stopping smoking is to die from it. This stark statement is supported by conclusive proof that smoking is the principal cause of some three million **premature** deaths in the world each year. Based on current trends, this figure could rise to ten million a year by 2030. One in two long-term smokers will die prematurely, half of them in middle age. Most die from one of the three main diseases linked to smoking: lung cancer, chronic lung disease (bronchitis and emphysema) and heart disease.

The grim reaper

The role played by tobacco smoking in causing deaths can be
spelled out in a bleak list of **mortality** statistics compiled by the
UK's Health Education Authority in 1998. Of the men who died
from lung cancer in 1995, 90 per cent (or 21,100 men) lost their
lives because of smoking. The figure for women was 73 per cent
(9500). Smoking was the principal cause of other deaths from
cancer of the throat and mouth, and cancer of the oesophagus.
There were similarly high figures for deaths caused by bronchitis
and emphysema – 86 per cent (15,100 individuals) of men and
79 per cent (9300) of women. Heart disease can be caused by
other factors, so the percentage of deaths linked to smoking
seems smaller. The overall totals, however, show the dangers:
26,300 men and 13,700 women died of heart disease brought
on by smoking. The British figures are representative of those in
most other countries.

Tobacco's history

The idea of smoking dried plant leaves is not new. The Vedic scriptures of India indicate that people were smoking various plants some 4000 years ago. It is likely that some of these plants included tobacco, although not the same type of plant that is used nowadays to produce cigarettes and other smoking products. The first people to smoke *Nicotiana tabacum*, which is the ancestor of modern tobacco, were the native people of North and Central America, where the plant grows naturally. The earliest real evidence of tobacco smoking comes from **artefacts** of the Maya civilization of Mexico, dating back about 1500 years.

Meeting of cultures

By the time the first Europeans arrived in the New World, about 500 years ago, tobacco smoking was common throughout all of North and South America. The Native Americans are now associated with the 'peace pipe' and other aspects of tobacco smoking, but they also used tobacco in other ways. It was common to chew and even eat the leaves, and people drank the juices of the plant. The Carib people of the West Indies – who gave the Caribbean its name – wrapped small tobacco leaves inside larger ones before smoking them.

This mixture was the forerunner of the cigar. European travellers to North and South America in the sixteenth century noted these uses of tobacco and tried most of them. It was the different methods of smoking that appealed to them, and many returned to Europe with samples of the new plant. The Portuguese, a seafaring and trading nation, were the first to cultivate the plant away from the Americas and to introduce it to the European public. However, it was only when tobacco arrived in England and France – in the 1550s and 1560s – that European tobacco cultivation began in earnest.

'Medicinal purposes'

At first Europeans viewed tobacco as a medicinal plant. In the mid-1500s it was used to treat a number of ailments, ranging from headaches to the common cold. English and French **herbalists** guarded their specimen plants jealously, much as they would for any medicine. Sir Walter Raleigh is often credited with being the 'father of tobacco smoking' and there is some truth to this view. In 1586 he sailed to England from the West Indies with a large supply of tobacco. His interest in the social, rather than the medical, side of smoking led to a boom in tobacco sales in Britain.

Ceremonial smoking of pipe tobacco was an established feature of Native American life when the first Europeans arrived in North America.

Tobacco's history

By the early 1600s pipe smoking was becoming widespread in London, Paris and other cities. Public houses sold tobacco, as did specialist shops, grocers and even goldsmiths. Not everyone, though, was pleased with this new habit. King James I of England issued a famous **denunciation** entitled *A Counterblaste To Tobacco* and increased the **tariff** on tobacco by 4000 per cent.

Growing trade

Despite the views of the English king and similar criticism by others in power, the public continued to demand more and more tobacco. Virginia, an English **colony**, proved to have an ideal climate to grow the plant, and huge **plantations** were developed there to supply the English market. Over the next few centuries, other European colonies began cultivating tobacco.

Up to the nineteenth century, pipe smoking and snuff remained the most common ways of taking tobacco in Britain. Then it was the turn of the cigarette, which became popular in Britain around the time of the Crimean War (1854–6). British soldiers saw their French and Turkish allies with cigarettes, and adopted the habit.

The first cigarettes were hand-rolled, either by the smoker or by specialist manufacturers. Then, in 1881 the automatic rolling machine was developed, enabling thousands of cigarettes to be produced in the same time it took to hand-roll dozens. The cost also dropped, which led to a huge rise in cigarette smoking by the early twentieth century. The results are borne out by looking at a simple Australian statistic: between 1908 and 1909 (the year that manufactured cigarettes were introduced to Australia), consumption of tobacco increased by more than 600 per cent.

Hollywood star Humphrey Bogart died of lung cancer brought on by years of smoking cigarettes.

❝(Tobacco) cures cancer of the breast, open and eating sores, scabs and scatches, however poisonous and sceptic, goitre, broken limbs…and many other things.❞

(Doctor Johannes Vittich in the early seventeenth century)

Public reaction

The United States turned to producing and smoking cigarettes at around the same time as Britain, the early 1900s. Before that, most US tobacco manufacturers had concentrated on processing tobacco for chewing, which today is a dwindling habit confined mainly to the American South.

The big boom

The popularity and huge sales of cigarettes turned the tobacco industry into big business. Individual firms became household names around the world. The big players in this development were companies based in the United States and in Britain. Some of the major tobacco companies, which are still widely known today, had grown from their roots as individual shops. The biggest tobacco company today is Philip Morris, which regularly chalks up annual profits of $5 billion or more. Its origins were in a small tobacco shop in London's Bond Street, opened by the original Philip Morris in the early 1850s.

Cigarette manufacturers saw sales and profits rise regularly through the decades of the twentieth century. One survey in 1948 found that 82 per cent of British men smoked regularly. Sales of cigarettes also rose, reaching a peak in 1960, when it was estimated that 40 per cent of US adults were smokers. Then things began to change.

And the bust?

Apart from signalling the high-water mark for US smoking, the 1960s saw the first major reaction to the tobacco industry. The public began to hear about research linking smoking with cancer, heart disease and other potentially **fatal** illnesses. Other reports suggested that tobacco companies manipulated levels of nicotine – the drug that produces **dependence** – to keep people hooked on tobacco.

Increased public awareness about these issues, and others such as **passive smoking**, have led to many restrictions on smoking in public places. Detailed studies, such as the 1997 report by Australia's National Health and Medical Research Council, indicate that households with at least one smoker run nearly a third greater risk of lung cancer and heart disease than non-smoking households. In other **developed countries**, such as the United States and the UK, overall numbers of smokers have fallen dramatically since the 1960s. In the **developing world**, however, the story is very different.

Cigarette smoking is a way of life in many parts of the world, even if it is declining in developed countries.

Who smokes and why?

Cigarette smoking is often – and rightly – described as an ugly habit. Nicotine-stained fingers, bad breath, constant coughing and the smell of stale tobacco make an unpleasant picture. All these factors, coupled with the now well-publicized health risks, would seem to make a persuasive case for not smoking. However, people still do smoke and young people are still turning to tobacco. Why?

Government **public health** officials, medical researchers and concerned anti-smoking organizations have been trying to discover the factors that lead people to smoke, and then keep them smoking once they have developed the habit. So far they have discovered that two important elements are age and **socio-economic** position, what is often more loosely described as someone's 'social class'. The factors that lead young people to smoke are discussed on pages 30–33; the following information relates to the elements in society as a whole which are most likely to smoke, or *least* likely to give up.

Occupational hazard

There is a definite link between smoking and socio-economic group. People involved in professional jobs, such as lawyers and accountants, are far less likely to smoke than those who work in **manual** trades. Some 1996 UK statistics relating to this are clear-cut. Using a scale that puts 'professional people' at one end and 'unskilled manual' at the other, researchers added groupings such as 'intermediate non-manual', 'junior non-manual', 'skilled manual' and so on. Plotted against these categories are the percentages of each group who smoke. The results show that 17 per cent of 'professionals' smoke, with the next group being 21 per cent, then 22 per cent and so on until 'unskilled manual' shows a figure of 38 per cent. Researchers who have studied these findings have concluded that although the overall trend in smoking has been a decline since the 1970s, this decline has been slowest among manual workers. Another case where the decline in smoking shows up in different ways is between the sexes.

Since the early 1980s cigarette smoking has declined by ten per cent for men but only six per cent for women. There is a danger that people can become swamped with such statistics, but they do point out areas for future concern. For whatever reason, the anti-smoking message seems to be less effective for people involved in unskilled trades and for women. Health policies must address this problem.

A day in the life of a smoker

Smoking is a day-long habit. One-third of all smokers have their first cigarette within fifteen minutes of waking up. Smoking this first cigarette is a ritual for the **dependent** smoker, then there are other 'landmarks' throughout the day that call for lighting up. Calmed by the first cigarette, the smoker sets about their business – but remains constantly alert about how, when and where the next cigarette can be smoked.

Many workplaces are non-smoking, so the smoker will need to go to a special area – sometimes simply the office fire escape – to feed the habit.

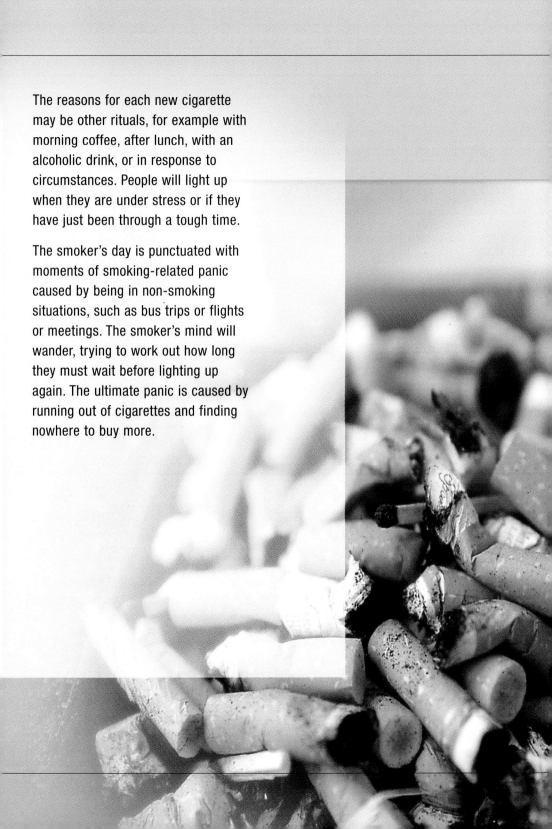

The reasons for each new cigarette may be other rituals, for example with morning coffee, after lunch, with an alcoholic drink, or in response to circumstances. People will light up when they are under stress or if they have just been through a tough time.

The smoker's day is punctuated with moments of smoking-related panic caused by being in non-smoking situations, such as bus trips or flights or meetings. The smoker's mind will wander, trying to work out how long they must wait before lighting up again. The ultimate panic is caused by running out of cigarettes and finding nowhere to buy more.

Across the generations

No matter how much we learn about health risks and the inconvenience caused to others, smoking remains firmly **entrenched** in most societies. Cigarette advertising has long since left the cinema and television screens but images of people smoking are still common. These images reinforce the message that smoking is 'cool' or 'sophisticated', or at the very least send out signals that it isn't all that harmful after all.

Unlike other dangerous drugs – and deaths from heroin and cocaine are relatively few compared with those caused by smoking – tobacco is widely available. There is no secrecy about buying it. Cigarettes and other tobacco products are sold in many shops and in coin-operated vending machines in pubs, restaurants and other public places. Although laws control the sale of tobacco to young people, it is still relatively easy for anyone to get regular supplies of cigarettes.

Powers of persuasion

More than for almost any other drug, a person's **conditioning** about smoking – whether to smoke or not – is developed in childhood. Very young people are extremely **impressionable** and the examples they see around them are important formative influences. Children are three times as likely to begin smoking if both of their parents smoke. Almost as important – if less provable with statistics – is the influence of siblings and friends. Children are more likely to smoke if these close companions set the example.

Attitudes, both in the home and in society at large, play a large part. Again, it is hard to quote statistics, but it is recognized that children growing up in households that disapprove of smoking are far less likely to smoke than those whose families approve or have no strong feelings. Parents who smoke – but who disapprove of their children's smoking – are in an awkward position. Their own sense of authority is threatened since they do the very thing that they are strongly warning their children against. The 'do as I say, not as I do' approach has side-effects in a wide range of other family matters, and the core conflict about smoking fuels the problem.

Across the generations

Advertising, which tries to manipulate public opinion, is also effective on the young. One study of secondary-school children found that a minority of smokers (38 per cent) but a majority of non-smokers (56 per cent) believed that tobacco advertising had a significant effect on influencing young people to start smoking. Other statistics show that children tend to smoke the brands of cigarette that are advertised most heavily.

Dangerous outcomes

Surveys indicate that the market for tobacco has become **saturated** in most **developed countries**. Tobacco manufacturers, like other manufacturers are always concerned about increasing sales. They realize that they must concentrate on young people, to preserve sales in the future. The alarming American statistics about the increase in smoking among the young (see page 11) seem to be typical of the position in other countries.

Using similar UK statistics, some alarming results emerge. More than a billion cigarettes a year are smoked by eleven- to fifteen-year-olds in the UK alone. They are spending £120 million in the process. If today's trends continue, according to a World Health Organization report, smoking will kill one million of today's teenagers and children in the UK before they reach middle age.

"We think it is advertising and promotional materials which affect and influence younger smokers. The tobacco industry needs 300 new smokers a day just to keep level and to replace the smokers who die."

(Spokesman for ASH, the anti-smoking pressure group, referring to the UK market)

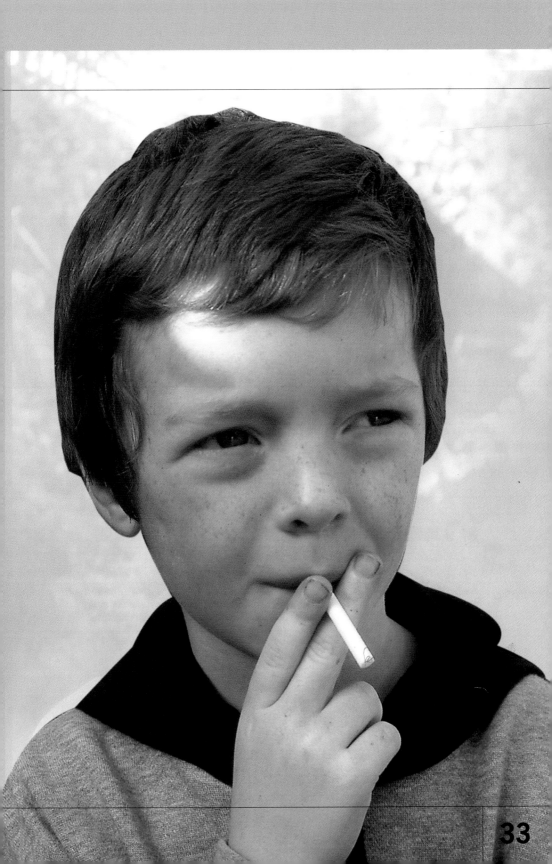

The initial cost

There are many arguments about the financial cost of smoking. The actual price of a packet of cigarettes – usually packaged in 20s although sometimes in tens – varies from country to country. Some of these differences are linked to simple economics. The cost is lower in countries or regions where tobacco is grown and cigarettes are produced. In America's prime 'tobacco country' of Virginia and North and South Carolina, for example, the price of a pack of cigarettes can be up to 40 per cent lower than in neighbouring states.

'Sin taxes'

The main cause of the difference in price, from one country to another, is the amount of **duty** that governments impose on the sale of tobacco. A proportion of the cost of each packet of cigarettes, cigars or other tobacco products goes straight to the government. Sometimes these duties are called 'sin taxes', since part of the government's aim is to control the use of a harmful product. Alcohol is usually subject to similar duties. Vast amounts of money are raised by these duties.

Many anti-smoking experts believe that governments now rely on them so much that they cannot make a genuine effort to crack down on smoking. In the UK, for example, tobacco duties generate about £9 billion a year.

Depressing arithmetic

Although affordable by most adults, the price of a single packet of cigarettes is still quite high. Maintaining a smoking habit, which will usually demand far more than one packet a week, is very expensive. By its very nature, smoking is a repetitive activity and frequent purchases are necessary. Taking Britain as an example – where the price of a packet of cigarettes in 2000 is £4.20 – it is possible to calculate the cost of smoking over one, two or more years. A person smoking a packet a day, which is not uncommon for people who smoke regularly, will spend £1394 in a year. Over 20 years the smoker will have spent £27,886, without allowing for future increases in price.

34

The tobacco industry

Tobacco is big business, and has been since the early seventeenth century when King James I of England combined disapproval (in his famous *Counterblaste*, see page 22) with keen business sense (by increasing the **tariff** on tobacco). Not surprisingly, American companies lead the world in tobacco sales and profits. Among the world leaders, however, are several British companies. The present situation results from a series of mergers and take-overs, involving American and British companies, at the end of the nineteenth century and the beginning of the twentieth.

Varied interests

Philip Morris, an American firm, is the world leader and claims about twelve per cent of world tobacco sales. Its multi-billion dollar annual profits allow it to maintain its market share, either through extensive advertising or in savage **price wars** with competitors in the United States. Marlboro, the leading Philip Morris brand, is estimated to be the world's most **lucrative** brand of any product. The second largest international tobacco company is BAT Industries. As with Philip Morris, the statistics relating to this corporate giant are staggering.

Like many other famous people, former US President, Ronald Reagan advertised cigarettes when he was a leading Hollywood actor.

I'M SENDING CHESTERFIELDS to all my friends. That's the merriest Christmas any smoker can have — Chesterfield mildness plus no unpleasant after-taste

Ronald Reagan

see RONALD REAGAN starring in "HONG KONG" a Pine-Thomas Paramount Production Color by Technicolor

CHESTERFIELD *Buy the beautiful Christmas-card carton*

BAT controls more than half of the cigarette market in 31 countries and produces nearly 600 billion cigarettes world-wide each year. Both of these companies, along with other giants such as Rothmans International, dominate the Australian market. In Australia, as in other areas, the firms have paid vast amounts both in advertising and in supporting research that tries to dismiss the dangers of smoking.

The other factor shared by these tobacco giants is the way in which they have **diversified** their business activities. This is a common practice for any type of large corporation, but tobacco firms have additional motives for 'spreading the load'. One reason is the decline or stagnation in the tobacco markets of the **developed countries**. (The position in **developing countries** is different: see pages 40–41.) Another is more practical: each further legal restriction on tobacco advertising or public smoking makes the prospect of an outright ban, at some time in the future, seem more likely.

Philip Morris and BAT, like other international tobacco companies such as R J Reynolds, Rothmans International and Imperial Tobacco, have bought out a number of non-tobacco-related companies. For example, BAT's other main UK involvement is in financial services: the company owns Eagle Star and Allied Dunbar. Philip Morris owns the large Miller Brewing Company in the United States as well as Kraft Foods. This combination of interests earns Philip Morris sales of more than $50 billion a year. Imperial Tobacco is the seemingly unlikely owner of the Seven Seas vitamins and fish oils.

The tobacco industry

Targeting women

Despite their entry into other fields, tobacco companies have not lost track of their traditional markets. Like **public health** officials and anti-smoking campaigners, they have seen all the statistics indicating an overall decline in smoking in the developed countries since the **Second World War**. Within this general downswing, however, is evidence that women might be an effective target for tobacco marketing.

Since the 1970s, tobacco companies have aimed a large portion of their advertising at women. Some brands are even designed with women in mind. Aware that the proportion of women smokers had increased after the Second World War, tobacco firms played on the fact that smoking represented a sort of **emancipation** for women. 'You've come a long way, baby', read the advertising slogan for one of these brands launched in the 1970s.

The year 1972 marked the peak in the number of women smokers, with a steady decline since, although not as fast as the decline among men. The good news for tobacco firms, though, is that young women, particularly in the sixteen to twenty-year-old range, are smoking more. A major reason for this is sex appeal – the feeling that smoking keeps people thin. According to one major fashion magazine in 1993: 'So long as thinness is equated with sexual attractiveness in women they will continue to smoke, whatever the risks. It is proven that people will risk death for sex.'

❝We also think that consideration should be given to the hypothesis that the high profits additionally associated with the tobacco industry are directly related to the fact that the customer is dependent on the product.❞

(BAT internal memo, 1979)

Tobacco advertising in the 1970s tried to link cigarette smoking with the efforts to promote equality for women.

In 1909, Mrs. Randolph Birch discovered that the laundry room was the best place to have a cigarette without her husband finding out. Mr. Birch suddenly discovered he had cleaner shirts.

You've come a long way baby.

VIRGINIA SLIMS.

Slimmer than the fat cigarettes m

VIRGINIA SLIMS
FILTER

Warning: The Surgeon General Has Determined That Cigarette Smoking Is Dangerous to Your Health

1.1 mg. nicotine—Menthol; 18 mg. tar, per cigarette, FTC Report Aug. 71

Pantsuit by Something! by Oscar de LaRenta.

"We can't defend continued smoking as 'free choice' if the person is addicted."

(US Tobacco Institute spokesman, 1980)

The world market

The tobacco industry has other strategies to deal with the problems it faces in the **developed world**. Chief among them is the development of new markets around the world. The last 40 years have seen a massive expansion overseas. In the 1960s the main growth area was South America. In the 1970s the tobacco giants turned their attention to the Middle East, Asia and Africa.

Target Africa

Africa has proved to be a real growth market for the tobacco giants. Sales there climbed by a staggering 33 per cent in the 1970s alone. The marketing drive was aided by advertising techniques that would never be allowed in these companies' home countries. In effect, the industry promoted the line that smoking builds brain power, physical strength and social approval. One brand was advertised in Malawi – one of Africa's poorest countries – by showing a packet of cigarettes on the top of an expensive Jaguar car. The message was obvious – our brand of cigarette lets you enter this exclusive world. Brand names used in Kenya include Varsity and Sportsman, which also suggest a world of glamour and prestige.

The problems faced by these countries are not limited to the smokers. Local farmers are encouraged to grow tobacco, a plant that is prone to many diseases. During its three-month growing period, tobacco needs up to sixteen applications of fertilizer, **herbicide** and **pesticide**. The next stage, the **curing** process, uses up vital supplies of wood and other fuels.

Looking east

The 1990s saw a huge growth of international tobacco sales in the former Soviet Union and other countries of Eastern Europe. Local people have always been avid smokers – consuming 700 billion cigarettes a year – and the major western firms are beginning to cash in. Companies use all sorts of techniques to build demand. One company working in Hungary offered free sunglasses to anyone who took a cigarette and smoked it in front of the publicity girl. The aggressive techniques seem to have worked. Western tobacco firms now control over half of the Eastern European market, up from only three per cent in 1988.

Large cigarette advertisements are prominent features in public places throughout Africa.

Drink Nestlé **MILO**
Fortified food drink
FOR HEALTH AND ENERGY

MAGGI CUBE

Embassy
Smooth all the way

Em

ff It's trench warfare – hand to hand combat. JJ

(A Reynolds executive, describing tobacco competition in Eastern Europe)

The 'other' tobacco industry

The tobacco industry, as it is normally defined, generates billions of pounds in profits each year, as well as significant amounts of tax money for various governments. Smoking, however, has a number of other effects on the economy, and nearly all of them are negative. The actual illnesses and other health complications resulting from smoking are outlined on pages 16–19; the cost in terms of money is dealt with here.

Hidden costs

Industry in general loses a great deal of money each year because of the smoking habits of employees. Most of this lost money is related to a decline in **productivity**, which results from 'workers taking smoking breaks' or **absenteeism** linked to smoking-related illnesses. In addition, there are the known side-effects of **passive smoking**, which can lead to bad feeling between smokers and non-smokers in a workplace. On top of these factors is the extra cleaning and maintenance costs that result from smoking.

Smoking also leads indirectly to huge costs arising from fires. The British Home Office compiles statistics about the causes of fires, and cigarettes and other smoking materials are major factors. In 1997, for example, smokers' materials were the third most common cause of accidental fires in homes – a total of 6498 fires. In that same year smokers' materials (other than matches) caused 185 deaths and 2383 non-**fatal** casualties in Britain.

A government bargain?

It is certainly true that some 80 per cent of the cost of a packet of cigarettes in Britain is tax. However, this is not 'money for nothing'. The Health Education Authority estimates that the UK's National Health Service spends about £1.5 billion a year in treating diseases caused by smoking. Other costs, which are less easily calculated, include the payment of sickness or invalidity benefits to people suffering from such diseases. In addition there is the payment of widows' pensions and other family social security benefits to the **dependants** of those who die as a result of smoking.

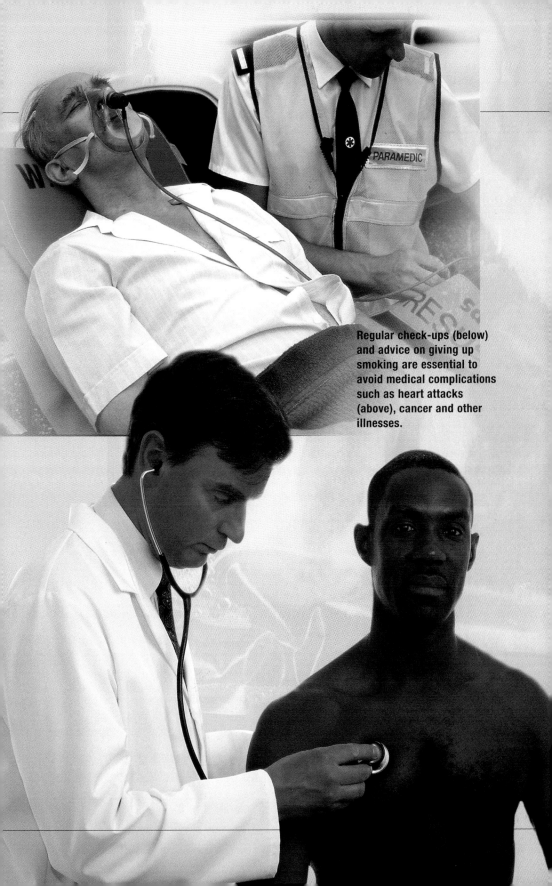

Regular check-ups (below) and advice on giving up smoking are essential to avoid medical complications such as heart attacks (above), cancer and other illnesses.

Legal matters

In most countries, the tobacco industry faces many legal regulations controlling how tobacco products are manufactured, sold, marketed and advertised. Most countries have an outright ban on cigarette advertising on television and in cinemas. Cigars and pipe tobacco, as well as 'smokeless tobacco' such as snuff and chewing tobacco, sometimes face fewer restrictions. The main thrust of most national laws is to control the spread of smoking among young people. In the UK the present law covering young people's smoking is the Children and Young Persons (Protection from Tobacco) Act 1991. Under this law it is illegal to sell any tobacco product to anyone under the age of sixteen. The Act increased existing fines for those who do sell to underage children to £2500. On average there are 140 prosecutions each year, with average fines of between £50–350. In Australia, advertising is strictly controlled and all tobacco products must carry health warnings. In some states it is illegal to sell to anyone under 18 years of age, in others under 16 years.

In the courts

The tobacco industry faces a potentially greater threat from **lawsuits** from individuals or groups of people whose lives have been damaged by smoking. In March 1997, for example, a US court ruled that the Philip Morris Company had to pay $81 million to the family of Jesse Williams, who had died of lung cancer after smoking regularly for 43 years. About $1.5 million of this was compensation to the family; the rest was described as **punitive damages** because of misleading advertising about the risks of smoking.

In July 1999 it was announced that a group of Australians who had suffered similarly would launch a **class action** suit against several major tobacco companies. The class action approach offers these people 'strength in numbers' to offset the power of the tobacco companies to pay for legal proceedings.

The biggest suit yet was filed by the US government against the major US tobacco companies. The suit claims some $20 billion in damages, a figure that represents the amount of government money spent on health care in treating tobacco-related illnesses. The US Attorney General Janet Reno argued that for many decades the companies tried to trick the public into thinking that cigarette smoking posed no health threat.

Tobacco imports face high taxes, which has led to a problem of smuggling. UK customs officials discovered cigarettes hidden in a shipment of footballs.

"If these claims succeed, then the total compensation will number in billions of dollars."

(Peter Gordon, the lawyer representing the ex-smokers in the Australian class action suit)

Treatment and counselling

It is important to realize that smoking is a habit that almost always leads to **dependence** in the user. Nearly every adult smoker, most of whom would like to quit, began as teenagers or even younger. At this age, people should really be discouraged from taking up smoking, or encouraged towards positive action to stop if they are already smokers. Willpower and determination underlie nearly every technique for quitting, but many people find it helpful to contact an anti-smoking organization for advice and specific tips. Many such organizations are listed on pages 52–53, and they provide a helpful springboard for kicking the habit.

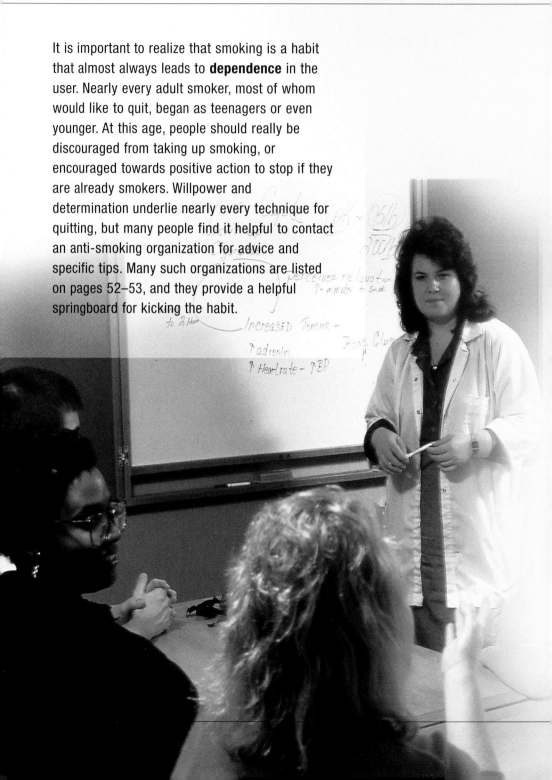

The youth focus

Karl Brookes is Project Manager with Action on Smoking and Health (ASH), a London-based anti-smoking organization with links to similar organizations around the world. ASH is at the forefront of raising public awareness about all the risks related to smoking, including those that lead to death as well as non-life-threatening conditions. ASH can also counter many of the claims made by the tobacco industry in its efforts to play down the risk of dependence on nicotine.

'Young people are a special case,' says Brookes. 'We can spend a lot of time and effort telling them how smoking has more than 50 ways of making life a misery through illness and more than 20 ways of killing you, and yet they are often inclined to brush aside these arguments.' This view is echoed by other researchers, who have found that many young people think of **fatal** illnesses as occurring only in adults. 'Ultimately, we're trying to get the no-smoking message across and we're realistic enough to accept that the "fatal illness" argument might not be the most persuasive to a teenager. The negative effects on appearance and the way smoking ages you (see pages 16–19) are more likely to have an effect. And who would want to continue smoking after their boyfriend or girlfriend said they don't like kissing an ashtray?'

Giving up

There are many methods of giving up smoking, from hypnosis to acupuncture. Describing all of them would take up more space than is available in this book. Generally, though, they fall into two categories – those simply involving willpower or behaviour and those that rely on special aids. Many of these aids take the form of nicotine substitutes which gradually lower the body's need for nicotine, once the first step of stopping smoking has been taken. They come in the form of nasal sprays, gums, patches, tablets and capsules. They either use the nicotine-reduction approach or have an additive such as silver acetate which makes cigarettes taste disgusting.

Those people who choose not to use such aids often concentrate on dealing with the 'activity' of smoking. They see the rituals associated with smoking – the morning cigarette, smoking after a meal and so on – as the big barrier. Many of these ex-smokers find some sort of replacement activity such as sucking on mints or chewing gum to take the place of smoking.

The right frame of mind

Whatever approach people take, successful quitters agree that it is important to approach the task with the right frame of mind. It is probably better not to concentrate on the negative side – the great sacrifice of not smoking – but to find positive goals, such as improved health or **self-esteem**. As the initial difficulties ease off, an activity such as running a mile or hill-climbing, that would have been difficult to do previously, can be helpful. This offers positive reinforcement, as does the boost of spending 'cigarette money' on more pleasant purchases.

ʄʄThere is absolutely nothing to giving up...there is no genuine pleasure or crutch in smoking. It is just an illusion, like banging your head against a wall to make it pleasant when you stop.ʃʃ

(Author Allen Carr, who formerly smoked 60 cigarettes a day)

Products designed to help people give up smoking usually provide nicotine in one form or other: clockwise, from top, chewing gum, lozenges, pills, skin patches and a pen-shaped 'cigarette substitute'.

People to talk to

Smoking is an ugly activity despite the reputation it has for being 'cool' or 'sexy'. Like so many other drugs that lead to **dependence** in later years – alcohol is a good comparison – nicotine, in the form of cigarettes, takes hold of the young when they are most **impressionable**. And as is the case with these other drugs, young people are not naturally drawn to smoking because it seems pleasurable in itself. It is usually **peer pressure** that provides the first push towards smoking.

Other voices

It is important to overcome the temptation to be swayed into smoking just because you think it will make you as thin as a supermodel or as sexy as a 'tough guy' film star. Try to make time to listen to other people about smoking, particularly ex-smokers or anyone involved in the medical world. The stories are very different from the glamorous image conveyed by tobacco advertisers and old films, where everyone seemed to have a cigarette dangling from their lips.

A doctor, pharmacist or health visitor is a good person to approach for informed and confidential advice about smoking. Most of these people can outline the negative side of smoking in great detail, often putting it in a local context by referring to a neighbour or local notable who is fighting the effects of lung cancer or heart disease as a result of smoking.

Checklist of queries

Before approaching anyone for advice about smoking, think about the areas where you might be confused or have heard only sketchy details. It might be to do with the risk of gaining weight if you stop smoking, or about the suitability of a method of quitting that costs a lot of money. You could also ask whether they believe that a substitute habit would be useful. Remember, the answer to any one of these queries might be the kick start in the fight to give up smoking, and the road to a healthier life.

Information and advice

Local libraries, doctors' surgeries and health centres are the best places to begin looking for information about tobacco and about giving up smoking. Most communities – even small villages – have support groups for those who are trying to quit the habit. One of the best, most comprehensive sources of up-to-date information about smoking is the Internet. You can use a home computer or one in your local school or public library to access dozens of useful home pages relating to the whole issue of smoking. Action on smoking and Health (ASH, see pages 46–47) is a good starting point. Its home page (http://www.ash.org.uk) has links to many organizations trying to build public awareness about the dangers of smoking and how to stop.

ISDD (Institute for the Study of Drug Dependence), Waterbridge House, 32–36 Loman Street, London SE1 0EE Tel: 020 7928 1211 www.isdd.co.uk
The ISDD has the largest drugs reference library in Europe and provides leaflets and other publications. SCODA (the Standing Committee on Drug Abuse) is located at the same address (tel: 020 7928 9500) and is one of the best UK contacts for information on drugs.

National Drugs Helpline
Tel: 0800 776600
The Helpline provides a free telephone contact for all aspects of drug use and has a database covering all of the British Isles for further information about specific drugs or regional information.

Quitline
Tel: 0800 002200
This free telephone service provides practical help and advice on how to stop smoking.

Youth Access
1A Taylors Yard, 67 Alderbrook Road, London SW12 8AD, Tel: 020 8772 9900
Youth Access is an organization which refers young people to their local counselling service. It has a database of approximately 350 such services throughout the UK.

Contacts in the United States

Child Welfare League of America
440 First Street N.W., Washington, DC 20001, Tel: 202/638-2952
www.cwla.org
The Child Welfare League of America, based in Washington, provides useful contacts across the country in most areas relating to young people's problems, many of them related to drug involvement.

DARE America
PO Box 775, Dumfries, VA 22026
Tel: 703/860–3273
www.dare-america.com
Drug Abuse Resistance and Education (DARE) America is a national organization that links law-enforcement and educational resources to provide up-to-date and comprehensive information about all aspects of drug use.

Youth Power
300 Lakeside Drive, Oakland, CA 94612, Tel: 510/451–6666, ext. 24
Youth Power is a nationwide organization involved in widening awareness of drug-related problems. It sponsors clubs and local affiliates across the country in an effort to help young people make their own sensible choices about drugs, and to work against the negative effects of peer pressure.

Contacts in Australia
ADCA

PO Box 269, Woden, ACT 2606
www.adca.org.au
The Alcohol and other Drug Council of Australia (ADCA), based in the Capital Territory, gives an overview of drug awareness organizations in Australia. Most of their work is carried out over the Internet but the postal address provides a useful link for those who are not on-line.

Australian Drug Foundation
409 King Street, West Melbourne, VIC 3003, Tel: 03 9278 8100
www.adf.org.au
The Australian Drug Foundation (ADF) has a wide range of information on all aspects of drugs, their effects and the legal position in Australia. It also provides handy links to state- and local-based drug organizations.

Centre for Education and Information on Drugs and Alcohol
Private Mail Bag 6, Rozelle, NSW 2039
Tel: 02 9818 0401 www.ceida.net.au
The Centre for Education and Information on Drugs and Alcohol is the ideal contact for information on drug programmes throughout Australia. It also has one of the most extensive libraries on drug-related subjects in the world.

Further reading
Buzzed, by Cynthia Kuhn, Scott Swartzwelder and Wilkie Wilson; New York and London: W.W. Norton and Company, 1998

Drugs, by Anita Naik, part of Wise Guides Series; London: Hodder Children's Books, 1997

Drugs: The Facts, HEA leaflet; London: Health Education Authority, 1997

Drugs Wise, by Melanie McFadyean; Cambridge: Icon books, 1997

A Primer Drug Action, by R.M. Julien; San Francisco: W.H. Freeman, 1995

Taking Drugs Seriously, A Parent's Guide to Young People's Drug Use, by Julian Cohen and James Kay; London: Thorsons, 1994

The Score: Facts about Drugs, HEA leaflet; London: Health Education Authority, 1998

Glossary

absenteeism
unexpected absences from a workplace

addiction
another word for dependence

addictive
leading to dependence

artefact
things made by people, not naturally occuring things; could be pots, tools and jewellery

class action
a legal case brought by a group of people sharing a cause

colonies
overseas territories controlled by a powerful country

conditioning
becoming used to something by experience

curing
drying of leaves to prepare tobacco

denunciation
a strong criticism

dependants
people, such as children, who rely on someone else's income

dependence
the physical or psychological craving for something

dependent
relying on a substance

developed countries
the richer countries such as the United States and the UK, which have economies that are fully developed

developing countries/world
the poorer countries, mainly in Africa, Asia and South America

diversified
turning to other unrelated areas

duty
taxes charged on a product

emancipation
equality in society

entrenched
held strongly for a long time

fatal
leading to death

genetic
a characteristic or disease that is inherited from a parent

genus
one of the scientific categories used to group similar plants or animals

gratification
pleasure seeking

herbalists
gardeners who specialize in growing herbs

herbicide
a chemical used to kill weeds that attack crops

impressionable
easily persuaded

intractability
a stubborn refusal to change

lawsuits
cases against others in court

lucrative
earning large profits

manual
using the hands for a job

mortality
relating to death

passive smoking
inhaling the smoke that smokers exhale

peer pressure
the pressure from friends of the same age to
behave in a certain way

pesticide
a chemical to kill insects and other creatures
that attack crops

placebo
a treatment that deliberately contains none of
the substance being tested

plantations
large farms

premature
occuring before it would be expected to occur

price wars
deliberately dropping prices in order to force
others out of competition

processed
changed in some way before being sold

productivity
the efficiency of a company

public health
dealing with issues of health in society

punitive damages
money ordered by a court to be paid as a
punishment

reinforcer
something that persuades people to do more
of something

saturated
unable to absorb any more

Second World War
the war (1939–1945) between Germany, Japan
and their allies against Britain, the United States
and their allies

self-esteem
the sense of pride in oneself

septic
infected

socio-economic
relating to wealth and social position

sponsorship
paying for an activity in order to advertise
during it

stimulant
a drug that makes people more alert or
energetic

supple
easy to move, elastic

tariff
money charged by a government on goods
entering the country

tolerance
the way in which the body learns to accept or
expect more of a substance

withdrawal
negative physical effects of giving up a
substance

Index

A absenteeism 42
Action on Smoking and Health (ASH) 47
addiction 5, 12
advertising 10, 11, 17, 30, 32, 36, 37, 39, 40, 44
ageing effect 8, 16, 18, 47
alcohol 4, 7, 12, 34, 50
anti-smoking message 11, 28, 47
appearance, negative effects on 8, 16, 18, 47
attraction of smoking 4, 8
availability 30

B BAT Industries 36, 37
blood pressure 18
brands 6, 36, 40
bronchitis 18, 19

C cancers 8, 18, 19, 23, 25
ceremonial smoking 20, 21
chewing tobacco 9, 20, 24, 44
children and young people, smoking and 10, 11, 13, 26, 30, 31, 32, 44, 47
Children and Young Persons (Protection from Tobacco) Act 1991 44
cigarettes 6-7, 9, 10, 22, 24, 26, 30, 36, 50
cigars 9, 10, 20, 44
class acion suits 44
cocaine 4, 15, 30
compensation claims 44, 45
conditioning 31
consumption of tobacco, increasing 11, 22, 24
cost of smoking 16, 34

D death 5, 18, 19, 30, 32
dependence 4, 6, 7, 12, 13, 25, 28, 46, 50
developed countries, smoking in 25, 32, 37, 38, 40
developing countries, smoking in 25, 37, 40-1
diabetes 18
dizziness 12
dopamine 12, 15
duties 34, 42

E economic costs, tobacco-related 42
effects of smoking
on appearance 8, 16, 18, 47
health risks 4, 8, 10, 11, 16, 18, 25, 42, 43, 47
psychological 7
unpleasant side-effects 12, 26
emphysema 8, 18, 19
energy and alertness 7

F filter tips 7
first-time smokers 12

G genetic factors 8
giving up smoking 14, 15, 46, 48-9, 50

glamorous image of smoking 4, 16, 30, 40, 50

H habitual smokers 28-9
health costs, tobacco-related 42, 44
health risks 4, 8, 10, 11, 16, 18, 25, 42, 43, 47
heart disease 8, 18, 19, 25
heroin 4, 12, 15, 30
history of tobacco 20-5

I information and advice 50, 52

L lawsuits 44
legal issues 44-5

M medical uses 20
mortality statistics 18, 19

N nasal sprays 48
nausea 12
new market development 32, 38, 40
nicotine 4, 6, 7, 12, 13, 14, 15, 18, 25, 50
nicotine gum 14, 48, 49
nicotine patches 14, 15, 48, 49
nicotine substitutes 48, 49

O oral gratification 8

P passive smoking 8, 25, 42
peer pressure 50
Philip Morris 24, 36, 37, 44
pipe smoking 9, 22, 44
processing tobacco 6, 40
psoriasis 18
public awareness of health risks 5, 25, 47
public places, smoking in 25, 37

R Raleigh, Sir Walter 20
reinforcers 13
repiratory illnesses 8, 18, 19
replacement activity 48, 50
rituals associated with smoking 28, 29, 48

S snuff 9, 22, 44
socio-economics, smoking and 26, 28
sponsorship in sport 10, 11
stimulants 7, 12, 18

T tariffs 22, 36
tobacco growing 6, 22, 40
tobacco industry 5, 22, 24-5, 32, 36-41, 42, 44, 47
tolerance to the effects of nicotine 12
treatment and counselling 46-9

V vitamin A 18

W website information 52
weight gain/loss 14, 16, 38, 50
withdrawal symptoms 12, 14
women smokers 18, 28, 38-9